AROUND THE GLOBE

MUST SEE PLACES IN
AUSTRALIA

BABY PROFESSOR
EDUCATION KIDS

Speedy Publishing LLC
40 E. Main St. #1156
Newark, DE 19711
www.speedypublishing.com

✓ In Australia, there are more kangaroos than people.

✓ The city of Melbourne, Australia, used to be called Batmania.

✓ It is the 6th largest country in the world, occupying an entire continent of some 7.6 million square kilometres.

✓ Lake Hillier in Australia is a bright pink color and scientists aren't sure why.

✓ Vegetation covers nearly 7 million square kilometres or 91 percent of Australia.

✓ 24 rabbits that were introduced to Australia in 1859 had multiplied in number to over 2 million in ten years.

✓ There's a river in Australia called the "Never Never River."

Fraser Island is a heritage-listed island located along the southern coast of Queensland, Australia, approximately 200 kilometres north of Brisbane. A major landmark on Fraser Island is the shipwreck of the S.S. Maheno. The Maheno was built in Scotland in 1905 as a luxury passenger ship for the trans-Tasman crossing.

Adelaide is the capital city of the state of South Australia, in Australia and the fifth-largest city in Australia. Today, Adelaide is noted for its many festivals and sporting events, its food and wine, its long beachfronts, and its large defence and manufacturing sectors. The River Torrens is the most significant river of the Adelaide Plains and was one of the reasons for the siting of the city of Adelaide, capital of South Australia.

Byron Bay is a beachside town located in the far-northeastern corner of the state of New South Wales, Australia. The town has several beaches which are popular for surfing. It is a resort popular with both domestic and international tourists, including backpackers, who travel along the Australian coast; the scenery also attracts skydivers. The area is also noted for its wildlife, with the whale watching industry a significant contributor to the local economy.

Gold Coast is a coastal city in southeastern Queensland on the east coast of Australia. It is the second most populous city in the state, the sixth most populous city in the country, and the most populous non-capital city and cross-state metropolitan area in Australia. The city consists of 70 kilometres of coastline with some of the most popular surf breaks in Australia. Gold Coast has Australia's largest professional surf lifesaving service to protect people on the beaches and to promote surf safety throughout the community.

Perth is the capital and largest city of the Australian state of Western Australia. Perth was originally founded by Captain James Stirling in 1829 as the administrative centre of the Swan River Colony. Perth has the fifth greatest number of skyscrapers of any Australian city after Sydney, Melbourne, Brisbane and the Gold Coast.

Brisbane is the capital and most populous city in the Australian state of Queensland, and the third most populous city in Australia. Brisbane is named after the Brisbane River on which it is located, which in turn was named after Scotsman Sir Thomas Brisbane, the Governor of New South Wales from 1821 to 1825. Popular tourist and recreation areas in Brisbane include the South Bank Parklands, Roma Street Parkland, the City Botanic Gardens, Brisbane Forest Park and Portside Wharf.

Launceston is a city in the north of Tasmania, Australia at the junction of the North Esk and South Esk rivers where they become the Tamar River. Settled by Europeans in March 1806, Launceston is one of Australia's oldest cities and is home to many historic buildings. Launceston serves as the commercial hub for the north of Tasmania, and like many parts of the state, is becoming a major tourist centre. Launceston is home to the Queen Victoria Museum and Art Gallery, which was established in 1891.

Kuranda is a town on the Atherton Tableland in Far North Queensland, Australia. The town is surrounded by tropical rainforest which abundant with wildlife and popular amongst birdwatchers. Attractions in Kuranda include a bird aviary, butterfly sanctuary, wildlife rescue/rehabilitation centre, reptile park and koala sanctuary. Kuranda is also a major centre for opals and didgeridoos.

Port Douglas is a town in Far North Queensland, Australia. The town is situated adjacent to two World Heritage areas, the Great Barrier Reef and the Daintree Rainforest. Port Douglas was No. 3 on Australian Traveller magazine's list of 100 Best Towns In Australia. Numerous companies run daily trips from the marina to the outer reef and the Low Isles for scuba diving and snorkelling. Port Douglas is also well known for its many restaurants, walks, golf courses, and five star resorts.

Kangaroo Island is Australia's third-largest island, after Tasmania and Melville Island. Kangaroo Island is noted for its honey and its Ligurian honey bees. The island has the world's only pure-bred and disease-free population of this type of bee. Kangaroo Island is one of South Australia's most popular tourist attractions, attracting over 140,000 visitors each year.

Kakadu National Park is a protected area in the Northern Territory of Australia. The name Kakadu comes from the mispronunciation of Gaagudju, which is the name of an Aboriginal language formerly spoken in the northern part of the park. Kakadu is ecologically and biologically diverse. The diverse environments of Kakadu National Park supports a great array of animals, a number of which have adapted to particular habitats. Some animals in the park are rare, endangered, vulnerable or endemic.

Pemberton is a town in the South West region of Western Australia, named after original settler Pemberton Walcott. Viticulture is now widely established with many investment schemes buying up large areas of pastureland and converting to vineyards. Pemberton is surrounded by karri forest with five national parks within 20 minutes' drive and has plenty of rivers, streams and dams for recreation. Pemberton has a Mediterranean climate, with warm, dry summers and cool, rainy winters.

Barossa Valley is a valley in South Australia located 60 km northeast of the Adelaide city centre and which is notable as a major wine-producing region and tourist destination. The wine industry plays a major role in the Barossa, being the main source of employment for many residents. The many hectares of vineyard are the most distinctive feature of the area. The Barossa Valley is a rich source of some of the oldest Shiraz vines in the world.

Karijini National Park is a National Park centred in the Hamersley Ranges of the Pilbara region in northwestern Western Australia. The five gorges that flow north out of the park, the Bee Gorge, Wittenoom Gorge, Kalamina Gorge, Yampire Gorge, and Dales Gorge provide spectacular displays of the rock layers. The park is most notable for its four prominent gorges marked by waterfalls and water holes.

Nitmiluk National Park is in the Northern Territory of Australia, 244 km southeast of Darwin, around a series of gorges on the Katherine River and Edith Falls. Previously named Katherine Gorge National Park, its northern edge borders Kakadu National Park. The gorges can be explored by canoe and flat bottomed boat. In the dry season the gorges become separated as the level of the river falls. They are interconnected in the wet.

Blue Mountains National Park is a protected national park that is located in the Blue Mountains region of New South Wales, in eastern Australia. The Blue Mountains National Park is one of the most popular national parks in Australia. Activities for the visitor include short walks to lookouts above cliffs and waterfalls, overnight and longer walks to more remote areas of the park, canyoning, abseiling, rock climbing and mountain biking. It is also home to the world's steepest railway, the Katoomba Scenic Railway.

Phillip Island is an Australian island about 140 km south-southeast of Melbourne, Victoria. Named after Arthur Phillip, the first Governor of New South Wales, Phillip Island forms a natural breakwater for the shallow waters of the Western Port. The Penguin Parade at Phillip Island Nature Park, in which little penguins come ashore in groups, attracts visitors from all over the world.

Broome is a coastal, pearling and tourist town in the Kimberley region of Western Australia. Cable Beach is a 22 kilometres stretch of beach near Broome. Four wheel drive vehicles may be driven onto the beach from the car park. This allows people to explore the beach at low tide to a much greater extent than would be possible on foot. Sunset camel rides operate daily along the beach. Being situated on a north/south peninsula, Broome has water on both sides of the town.

Uluru also known as Ayers Rock, is a large sandstone rock formation in the southern part of the Northern Territory in central Australia. Uluru is an inselberg, literally "island mountain". An inselberg is a prominent isolated residual knob or hill that rises abruptly from and is surrounded by extensive and relatively flat erosion lowlands in a hot, dry region. Uluru is one of Australia's most recognisable natural landmarks. Uluru is notable for appearing to change colour at different times of the day and year, most notably when it glows red at dawn and sunset.

Canberra is the capital city of Australia. Canberra is a planned city and the inner-city area was originally designed by Walter Burley Griffin, a major 20th-century American architect. The native forest in the Canberra region was almost wholly eucalypt species and provided a resource for fuel and domestic purposes. A resident of Canberra is known as a "Canberran".

Melbourne is the capital and most populous city in the state of Victoria, and the second most populous city in Australia. Melbourne is rated highly in the areas of education, entertainment, healthcare, research and development, tourism and sports. Melbourne is an international cultural centre, with cultural endeavours spanning major events and festivals, drama, musicals, comedy, music, art, architecture, literature, film and television.

Cairns , is a regional city, founded in 1876, encompassing smaller townships in the far north of Queensland, Australia. The city was named after William Wellington Cairns, then-current Governor of Queensland. The Cairns region is the fourth-most popular destination for international tourists in Australia after Sydney, Melbourne and Brisbane. The Cairns esplanade includes a swimming lagoon with adjoining barbecue areas.

Darwin is the capital city of the Northern Territory, Australia. It is the smallest and most northerly of the Australian capital cities, and acts as the Top End's regional centre. Darwin was originally a pioneer outpost. Tourism is one of Darwin's largest industries. Darwin is a hub for tours to Kakadu National Park, Litchfield National Park and Katherine Gorge.